F*ck You Money!!!

The Guide to Firing Your Boss, and Hiring Yourself!

Cory The Author

ISBN-10: 1535163984
ISBN-13: 978-1535163989

Table of Contents

Introduction

"F*ck you money!!"- Is a stash of cash which will allow you to operate and live as a free human being rather than a slave.

Slave: a person who is strongly influenced and controlled by something

Wage slave: a person wholly dependent on income from employment, typically employment of an arduous or menial nature.

Across the globe a day doesn't go by without you hearing about record amounts of layoffs. The unemployment rate is high. So many people are desperate to keep their jobs that they'll take any kind of abuse from Corporate America. Most people may be only a few paychecks away from financial ruin without knowing it.

The game has changed. The players have changed. A man used to be able to work with the same company his whole life, make a good salary to support his family. It was a time when people didn't have to worry much about jobs going to China, or India coming to take jobs.

Today, you can lose your job with no guarantee of getting another any time soon. A college diploma really doesn't carry as much weight as it used to *unless you studied medicine, engineering, law, or computer science.*

We are caught up in a fiercely competitive struggle for wealth or power, or an exhausting, usually competitive routine known as the rat race. That routine leads to nothing but debt, and stress. You're just hustling for a weekend. Working from paycheck to paycheck. If you're going to be caught up in a fiercely competitive struggle for wealth or power, why not do it for yourself?

I remember Jim Carrey gave a commencement speech at the Maharishi University of Management. In the speech, Carrey put some things in perspective for the graduates:
"The decisions we make in this moment are based in either love or fear. So many of us choose our path out of fear disguised as practicality. What we really want seems impossibly out of reach and ridiculous to expect so we never ask the universe for it." And then, drawing on his own personal experience, particularly as a child, he offered this advice: *"I learned many, many lessons from my father, but not the least of which is that you can fail at something you don't want, so you might as well take a chance doing what you love."*

It is impossible to enjoy the riches, wealth, and abundance that life, this universe has to offer if you are working a 9-to-5 to "make a living." Most people spend the majority of their time slaving away at a 9-to-5 doing work that is meaningless. In society we are conditioned to believe that a job is "all there is," or that we have to "work hard" for money.

It's "what everybody else does" or "what our parents did." So we get comfortable being in this continuous cycle. *Everyone else is* – broke, poor, and in debt. You most likely will never experience true wealth or anything close to it in this lifetimes if you stay in this cycle.

Charles Bukowski, once said, *"How in the hell could a man enjoy being awakened at 6:30 am by an alarm clock, leap out of bed, dress, force-feed, shit, piss, brush teeth and hair, and fight traffic to get to a place where essentially you made lots of money for somebody else and were asked to be grateful for the opportunity to do so?"*

"When the entirety of your earnings are exhausted on food and shelter, your labors are no longer viewed as an opportunity for economic advancement, but rather as an act of self-preservation. In the real world, that's called Slavery." - unknown

"I freed a thousand slaves I could have freed a thousand more if only they knew they were slaves." - Harriet Tubman

Back then slaves were given shelter, food, and their basic needs - to pick cotton. Now the "slaves" work for the same basic needs shelter, food, water, and clothes.

"Slavery was never abolished. It was only extended to include all the colors" - Charles Bukowski

I recently came up with a strategy and game plan. I wanted financial freedom. I saved enough money to invest in myself so I could have an exit strategy. I felt enormously liberated at the idea of having a blank canvas to do whatever I liked for a whole year and also a little bit anxious about how I would fill my time. I gladly said "fuck you" to my asshole boss!!! Here's how you can do it.

Chapter 1
Hustling for a Weekend

You are dependent upon your job to keep a roof over your head, and food on your table. You are at the mercy of other people. You trade your time for *money*. This is the most inefficient way to make money, and you will never become wealthy working under such conditions. I for one, don't want to sit on my ass in a cubicle all day. I want to travel, and see the world. The average person's Monday to Friday is waking up early, and fighting traffic for two hours.

Then they head home and eat take-out because they're too tired to cook. They plop down in front of the TV because they're too exhausted to do anything else. Then they go to bed and repeat this same cycle. They put in reckless hours during the week. Many of them have all this money piled up, but they never really get to enjoy the fruits of their labor because their labor takes up most of their lives. Eventually this hatred will cause stress and in the long run, it will have lasting effects on their health.

I woke up one day and said *"Wait a minute! Why am I putting up with this shit?" "I want to do things my way."* When did we all get addicted to the "Kool-Aid"? Fuck this shit!! Each day you go to work put in 40 to 50 hours a week, and you contribute your time and effort to building someone else's dream.

The only way out is starting your own business. Of course, the demands and sacrifices of a business aren't for everyone. You'll likely end up with maxed-out credit cards and sleepless nights spent in front of a computer. Think about it. At some point in time, someone made up the idea that we are supposed to work for eight hours a day. You should be living out your dreams, not the dreams of somebody else.

The first step toward escaping the rat race is being able to *see* the rat race. When you're just trying to keep up with the joneses, it's easy to get caught up in wanting to have a big house, and an expensive car. More on this later…

"The more we value things, the less we value ourselves." – Bruce Lee

"Only the self-sufficient stand, alone. Most people follow the crowd and imitate." – Bruce Lee

The goal is to become self-sufficient. Self-sufficiency is a mindset. Perhaps the most difficult habit to break when striving for a self-sufficient life is changing the way you think about how you spend your money. Self-sufficiency is all about developing your own resources and being able to support oneself financially: independent, self-supporting and free from the influence, guidance, or control of others: The idea of self-sufficiency appeals to those of us who are rebelliously independent.

I firmly believe that being self-sufficient is one of the most important things a person can do. We rely on someone else for almost everything in our lives. You can create your own source of income. The more you can take care of yourself, the better off you'll be physically, financially, emotionally and even spiritually. Those that are self-sufficient financially find it to be empowering. It's the same idea with fuck you money.

Fuck you money is having of enough **money** to be financially independent. **You** can then say "**fuck you**" to an employer and it won't affect your livelihood. Being financially independent is priceless. You can't put a price tag on freedom.

The world is your oyster. You have the ability and the freedom to do anything or go anywhere. You are in a position to take the opportunities that life has to offer. You are the master of your fate. You are the director of your life. You have to think and direct your own life. It all starts with the way you think. People ask me, how do you live so freely without the stress of a 9-to-5? How do you go to all these different places around the world? You create your own circumstances. People are so used to thinking negatively. It's always I can't. Redirect your thoughts. Don't focus on what didn't work.

In your mind you prepare for failure, and when you prepare for something, that is usually what happens. Tell yourself how great you are. Be so sure about your abilities, and what you can do. You control your destiny. Do whatever you want to do. There's a certain freedom when you develop this mindset. The world is full of opportunities, so take advantage. As the captain of your life, you set the course of how you want it to go.

It starts with your mindset and focus. A job should be used as a stepping stone. An educational tool. For example, if you want to start your own law firm sometimes it helps to work at someone else's law firm to learn how to run your own. Look at a job as an **apprenticeship**.

Developing the right mindset is really crucial to succeeding in anything. When you're trying to transition from a job to entrepreneurship the right mindset is key. Your mindset is the sum of your knowledge, including beliefs and thoughts about the world and yourself in it. The way you think influences your self-esteem, your confidence, your creativity, your world-view. The right mindset can fire up your creativity, motivate and inspire you when the world doubts your genius. Visualize your success. If you constantly think, *"this isn't going to work. I'm never going to make any money"* then you are right. You must know it's going to work.

Commit to mastery. **There is a massive learning curve when you are free and ready to be an entrepreneur, and you're constantly pushed out of your comfort zone. Knowledge isn't power** until knowledge is applied. Then and only then, does it become powerful. To start a business, escape the rat race or invest. You have to be knowledgeable in those areas of life. Do research in what you're trying to achieve. **Your most useful tool therefore, will be research.** It is essential to be educated in what you're trying to achieve. It will help you operate without the hindrances of ignorance. It is sometimes better to seek expert guidance.

GET COMFORTABLE WITH BEING UNCOMFORTABLE...

The comfort zone - most people in society are stuck in one – with no way out. People stay where they are, because they're *comfortable*. People hold on to what they have, because it makes them *comfortable*. People buy things they don't need, because it feels *comfortable*. We let society tell us what to do, because we want to live a *comfortable* life.

In society, you're provided with a comfortable life. Whether you decide to opt-in or not is up to you. We depend on the government, and our boss, to handle our lives for us. Corporate employment is no more than a new method of slavery that is even more profitable for the ruling class.

Maybe we should develop our own self-reliance & evolve. Will we? Maybe it's time to say 'fuck it', and get out of your comfort zone. To move forward in life, we must get out of our comfort zone. I know it's easier said than done, but to get out of the rat race you have to be uncomfortable.

For example, someone that wants to lose weight or build muscle is going to feel some pain. And your own life is no different. The gym is just a metaphor for life. There would be no light without darkness; there is no growth without pain. The best lessons in life always come from pain.

Another thing to remember is comfort kills.
Being uncomfortable is a sign that you're growing and learning. People don't change until they are uncomfortable. In order to grow, you need to get comfortable with being uncomfortable. Fuck your morning coffee. Fuck your freshly ironed suit. Fuck your TV. Life is always moving – forever flowing. You need to move to stay alive. You need to evolve and change.

Most importantly don't let the idea of failure scare you. Most people see failure as the end of the world. Failure is about learning. Anytime you're starting out in a career or any endeavor there will be some failures. You can't get around failure, that's just a part of the game. There are some of us that dwell on failure. Motivation can grow from that setback. A loss will only make us better if we let it. A loss will teach you how to win if you let it. For example, any hero in a movie such as James Bond, Batman, or Luke Skywalker has always experienced a moment where it seems like they were losing. Then eventually they started winning. Learn from failure.

Write down your ideas and goals. I constantly have ideas, ideas for businesses, and ideas for books. A written goal brings clarity and focus. We often hear the hardest part of starting a business is the idea itself. A lot of those same great ideas are tossed away and never manifested. So write them down. Always remember "You can trade hours for dollars or ideas for millions." Also read. Read the *Aha Moment: The Guide to Creating a Game Changer*.

Chapter 2
Escaping the Corporate Plantation

To escape the plantation, you need a plan. To go to war you need a plan. Developing a game plan is important if you want to stay on track. A game plan is a strategy worked out in advance in business. A "game plan" is a strategy for attaining a goal. Ask any successful person how they became successful. They will tell you that they had a vision and developed a game plan to achieve that vision. Having a perfectly thought-out game plan is essential in business and sports. How do you create a game plan?

You need to start with a strategic plan that describes your vision, and mission. Creating a Game Plan is one of your first steps to escaping the rat race. A detailed game plan allows your mind to know what is possible, which removes some of the fear. It removes doubt, adds certainly, and puts you in a resonance that attracts new opportunities. You need a really clear and practical strategic plan.

Everyone should know anytime you start a new job you should have a plan. It could be to advance in that company or use that job as a way to save enough money and escape the rat race. Then you should have a strategy in mind. You should learn from the supervisors, managers, CEOs and other employees as well.

To escape the plantation, you also need strategy. Strategy describes where you want to go, not necessarily how you're going to get there. Unlike business plans, there is no one right way to create effective strategic planning. It is, by definition, brainstorming at its best. Since it depends on creativity and outside-the-box thinking, there is no perfect way to design a winning strategic plan.

A good strategy describes the general intention and uses that as the platform for taking action. Bear in mind that "intent" can change over time. No one knows what the future might bring. Circumstances change and when they do you might need to re-define your intent, sometimes radically. This is a normal part of strategy development. Managing your time as you prepare **to leave** the **plantation is very important.**

It is less specific than an action plan which tells who, what, when. Instead, it tries to broadly answer the question, "How do we get there from here?" Do we want to take the train? Fly? Walk? A good strategy will take into account existing barriers and resources people, money, power, materials, etc. It will also stay with the overall vision, mission, and objectives of the initiative. Often, an initiative will use many different strategies--providing information, enhancing support, removing barriers, providing resources, etc.--to achieve its goals.

Objectives outline the aims of an initiative--what success would look like in achieving the vision and mission. By contrast, strategies suggest paths to take and how to move along on the road to success. That is, strategies help you determine how you will realize your vision and objectives through the nitty-gritty world of action. So while you're at your job you should coming up with a strategic game plan and an exit strategy. Figure out the moves you need to make to get a clean break from your job.

Chapter 3
Invest in Yourself

Taking the time to invest in yourself, whether it is reading books about things you never knew about ...you are still learning something new. The more you learn the more you earn. Investing in yourself financially is a move that can set you up to make that move of leaving your job. You are the most important place you can put your time and money, and yet you are probably the one thing that tends to get neglected in life.

In order to be the best version of yourself, you have to work on yourself. Initially, that may seem selfish. Invest in things that will make you money. It takes money to make money. Some of us enjoy spending money on shoes, clothes, cars, and some of us really enjoy eating at nice restaurants. But some people don't want to spend money on tools that will potentially help them to earn more money.

Warren Buffett, one of America's wealthiest people, is famously followed for his investing views and strategies said it best The most important investment you can make is in yourself. Very few people get anything like their potential horsepower translated into the actual horsepower of their output in life. Potential exceeds realization for many people...the best asset is your own self.

When you invest in your personal development you take responsibility for your life, your circumstances and your happiness. You become the agent, the doer, and the effector. Shift your focus from "exchanging time for dollars" to "leveraging dollars for your dollars." In other words, let money work for you. Invest in things that will double your dollars.

Formal education can teach a lot about theory and a variety of different subjects. That said, education can only take you so far. At the end of the day, you need to eventually start doing things to truly become an expert.

Jim Rohn once said that a formal education can make you a living but self-education can make you a fortune. When you're working for yourself, you learn on the job so to speak.

Society tells us to become a zombie slaving away at a 9-to-5 so we can put food on the table. It's so easy to get caught up in the rat race but if you're itching to find your passion, it's time to make some changes and make it a priority.

Chapter 4
F*ck You Money

In the movie, The Gambler, a loan shark named Frank (played by John Goodman), explains the Position of F-You to gambler Jim Bennett, (played by Mark Walberg).
Fuck you money, as you may have guessed, is cash stashed away in your bank account, or mattress which you can use to live on when you need to say "fuck you!" to an asshole boss. Fuck you money is good because it gives you power and independence. When you have enough money put away you don't have to worry.

If you don't already have a stash of fuck you money, it's very important that you begin working on getting some as soon as possible. There are so many reasons to have f*ck you money. After you take care of the parasite of debt and downsize to a reasonable standard of living, start stacking that paper and building your "fuck you fund." Start a side gig and create multiple streams of income. Invest that money into income generating assets while living off your primary income.

Lose the brand new car, and pay cash for one. In a couple of years your debts will be gone. "Savers are losers! Don't just save money to hold on to it but save money to invest into something that will keep money circulating.

Here are three things you could do to save more than $100 a month: Cut cable TV and get Netflix. Make your food instead of always going out; and don't buy new clothes at the mall, but go to TJ Maxx or Marshall's instead. Or instead shop at your local Goodwill or thrift stores. Would you rather struggle for 3 to 5 years to gain financial freedom, or be broke for 40 years?

Flip your money. To "flip" money means to invest an amount in something in the hopes of making a whole lot more money than you invested. There are so many different assets you can flip. You can get into the house **flipping** game. When you first hear the word, "flipping," what immediately comes to mind? That's right, houses. We all know someone that finds houses, fixes them up, and then sells them for an overall profit. One way to use some of your fuck you money is flipping houses.

I'm sure you're familiar with assets and liabilities. Right? An asset is something which an individual owns. A liability is something which an individual owes. So your car and house are liabilities. Now if you have rental properties those would be considered assets. An asset generates cash flow.
Liabilities are financial obligations, or debts. In order to build wealth your focus should be on assets. Try to minimize liabilities. Once you develop this type of mindset you'll build wealth.

Like I mentioned before start a side hustle. I'm sure many of you are familiar with that term, but if not let me refresh your memory. *Side Hustle – Is a product or service that you offer or sell on the side of your current full-time job to earn extra income on the side.* So if you work full-time, but you cut grass on the weekends, that's a side hustle. Side hustling has been a game changer for many people.

The need for a side hustle could grow out of a goal, such as trying to quit your job. Maybe you're not ready to leave your full-time job and put it all on the line yet — but you still want to dedicate a solid amount of time each week to working on it. The game has changed. many nine-to-fivers have taken on second gigs to earn extra money or pursue their passions. Start your side hustle.

"Create the things you wish existed."
- Unknown

"If you don't find a way to make money while you're sleeping,
you'll work until you die."
- Unknown

Side hustle ideas:
1. Landscaping
2. Scrap metal collecting
3. Computer repair
4. Catering
5. Brokering (Connecting people with work)
6. Handy man
7. Creating and selling items
8. Coaching (sports/mentoring)
9. Transportation delivery
10. Buying and selling items
11. Moving and hauling junk
12. Street marketing (handing out flyers)
13. Pet sitting and dog walking

"I'd rather hustle 24/7 than slave 9 to 5."
– Unknown

"The dream is free. The hustle is sold separately."

Hustle like Hell

It's too many people looking for the hook up. Everybody wants the quick fix. That's why so many people play the lotto, or look for get rich schemes. Nobody wants to endure the struggle of actually building something. The cure for the struggle is to hustle. It's not enough to just hustle, but be consistent. You have to adopt the hustler's mentality. Go the extra mile. Talent isn't enough. You have to hit the ground running. If you fail, use it as a learning experience and keep grinding.

Hustle means going all out, every day, until you hit your breaking point – and then continuing on because hustle does not break. Talent does not decide your success but your hustle does. Hustling allows you to free range to utilize your work ethic, talents, network, and other resources. People don't hustle because of laziness or fear of failure.

Most of us simply look at successful individuals that made it and dream of being just as successful, but we don't realize the work they put in. We have excuses such as not having the natural talents or gifts so we never try. We do not have control over that, but you can control over how hard you hustle. The hustler puts it all on the line for as long as he needs to. There is no — I will try this for a month and see what happens. It is either all in or all out.

"Hustle in silence and let your success make the noise."
– Unknown

"Hustle until your haters ask if you're hiring."
- Unknown

"Hustle beats talent, when talent doesn't hustle."
- Unknown

"Without hustle, talent will only carry you so far."
– Gary Vaynerchuk

*"You can't have a million-dollar dream with a
minimum-wage work ethic."*
– Stephen C. Hogan

"Hustle until you no longer *need to introduce yourself."*

So, **wherever you are in the work force, you can still make the change**. Things will not get any better until you take action! **If you are unhappy with where you are**, then **make a move**, a better life, one where you are in control of what you do and when you do it.

You owe it to yourself to at least explore the opportunities that are out there and open to you? It's not just about "positive thinking." It is not enough that you *think* about what you want and phrase your affirmations in a way that you already have what you want – you have to legitimately *believe* and *know* that you already have what you want. Your mind and the universe do not know the difference between what you think is "real" or imagined; it is all the same. People say quite often, "I'll do it someday." What? Someday is never going to be here. The only day we have is Today.

Once you know what you want and you've affirmed it, know *why* it is that you want it. Imagine a situation in which you already have what you want. For example, maybe you have an idea. Picture that idea manifesting. Put that moment in your own mind, and don't hold back. If you spend all of your time thinking like this, instead of focusing on "how will I pay my bills this week?" or "I'm broke!" - you will start to see things turn around for you extremely quickly, and you will be well on your way to getting out of that job that is sucking the life *out* of you and, doing what you've always wanted to do.

Schools are not what they used to be. College grads are pouring coffee and still living at home. Retirement age has morphed from 65 to 6 feet under, till death does employment part.

We were raised with this idea that if we go to school, get a typical job, and make a lot of money, we will be happy. Happiness should be a reflection of your success, not by what kind of car, or how big your house is. I would rather struggle working towards something I love than working at a company that makes me miserable.

The longer you remain on a corporate plantation, the harder it will be to escape. The 9-to-5 cycle becomes so repetitive. Do not become a corporate slave; you need to go out and make your dreams come true. You will find that corporations in a capitalistic society are not very different from the slave owners of the earlier generations. If you're working for a corporation then do realize that it's a game. Read *The Prince* by Machiavelli, *Think and Grow Rich* by Napoleon Hill, *Rich Dad Poor Dad* by Robert Kiyosaki - just to name a few.

Information is knowledge and knowledge is power once action is applied — this is where it all starts. By doing what I want to do instead of what others want from me, I have been able to inspire others to follow their dreams. You will start to recognize the beauty that life have to offer.

Modern society bombards us with subtle messaging that shapes us into debt slaves. We are brainwashed into accepting debt. And since our current financial system constantly requires more debt to "stay alive," the system is therefore very much involved in shaping your thought process such that you stay in debt. In order to do anything, you must first "see" and recognize the problem.

Life should be lived as a vacation. When you are doing what you love you don't ever need a day off. To be successful, you need more than a financial education. You need **passion**. Chase your **passion** and the money will come. Chase money and you will never find your **passion**. When you feel **passionate** about what you are doing, you radiate energy and enthusiasm. A **passion** for what one is doing is an **important** first step in leading change.

Take action!!!! It's time to embrace the change, because it's happening whether you like it or not. So write down what you want to accomplish, and then create your game plan. From there create an exit strategy, and don't forget to have your Fuck you money stashed up!!!!! Would you rather have a J.O.B. (Just over broke) or be financially free to do your own thing? The choice is yours. Step forward and take action. When you do this, you will be closer to the force of the universe. Don't forget to be consistent. Too many people start something and don't finish it. Be fucking consistent. It's not the job you need, but the income. Find the income.

"Believe in your fucking self."
- Unknown

"One day your life will flash before your eyes. Make sure it's worth watching."
- Unknown

"My goal is to build a life I don't need a vacation from."
- Rob Hill Sr.

"He who is not courageous enough to take risks will accomplish nothing in life."
– Muhammad Ali

What have we learned today?

1. Save money (That's your fuck you money)

2. Develop the right mindset. (Entrepreneur mindset)

3. Develop a precise game plan. (Save money, start a side hustle, invest in knowledge and in an asset or business)

4. Develop an exit strategy. (Have a set amount of money you can survive off of, and hopefully your side hustle is already blooming from the seed you planted.)

5. Take action!! (All the other steps are in vein when action isn't taken.) Take a deep breath and take action.

<u>The cure for poverty:</u>

1. Cut the T.V. off

2. Read

3. Drop dead beats

4. Save 10% of your income to invest it.

5. Stop buying shit you don't need

"You get up two and a half million dollars, any asshole in the world knows what to do: you get a house with a 25-year roof, an indestructible Jap-economy shitbox, you put the rest into the system at three to five percent to pay your taxes and that's your base, get me? That's your fortress of fucking solitude. That puts you, for the rest of your life, at a level of fuck you. Somebody wants you to do something, fuck you. Boss pisses you off, fuck you! Own your house. Have a couple bucks in the bank. Don't drink. That's all I have to say to anybody on any social level. Did your grandfather take risks? I guarantee he did it from a position of fuck you. A wise man's life is based around fuck you. The United States of America is based on fuck you. You have a navy? Greatest army in the history of mankind? Fuck you! Blow me. We'll fuck it up ourselves".
  - The Gambler, a loan shark named Frank
(played by John Goodman)